An Attempted Translation of the Soul

Clare Galletta

BookLeaf
Publishing

India | USA | UK

Presentation by *BookLeaf Publishing*

Web: www.bookleafpub.com

E-mail: info@bookleafpub.com

ISBN: 9789363317024

First edition 2024

*To everyone. Because some way or another, all
that I have met have influenced my writing. To
my parents, who sat down and read every one
that I wrote and brought to them at eleven at
night or eight in the morning. To my sisters,, for
their endless, unquestioned support.*

ACKNOWLEDGEMENT

A special thanks to the teachers who showed me that a passion for literacy does not always have to stay in the confines of structured writing. That there is joy, humor, sorrow, and satire in all of it.

PREFACE

It does not have to be pretty. It does not have to make sense for everyone. Many times, what is felt so truly in one moment is contradicted in the next. Writing is sitting within yourself and sharing secrets between you and your soul.

*Content warning:
Topics of death, self-harm, and mental illness are referenced and depicted in a few poems. Please read with caution and kindness to your soul. Specific depictions mentioned in:
On Translating Love, pt. 3
On Translating Battling with Mental Illness

On Translating Love Pt. 1

What is love but a moment in time
And forever
All at once
Encapsulated in a rain drop
A smile
Pollen baskets on a bumblebee's legs.
What is love but everything
Grand gestures
Motive in war
But a kiss on the forehead
Or a nod of encouragement.
What is love but trust
A leap from a pools edge into open arms
Drifting to sleep on a friend's couch
Lending a hand
Accepting a hand.
What is love but the light of a candle
The light of the sun
The light of the moon
The light of our souls.
What is love but all we ask for.
All of every inch of skin and hitch of breath.
The depth between each goosebump.

Pt. 2

Love is ageless, shape shifting, and ever-present.
Love is bold. And quiet.
Love is its own language, often unspoken.
Simply known.
It is silly faces at age fourteen echoing into our
thirties.
It is memorized one-liners, and hearing the same
song in your heads at the same instant.
Love is listening. Hearing. Uplifting.
Fully enveloping. Being held by each other no
matter a five or two thousand mile distance.
It is full names, nicknames, toasts of wine,
whiskey, and pickle juice.
Love is soft. And fierce. And safe.
Love is an honor.
It is an honor to be loved by you.
Love is us

Pt. 3

I am ripped. Fear of what is around the corner
follows every 'I love you', and every new bond
fortified is tinged with a hint of murky knots.
I grasp on to each moment with all of my might,
when will it go? When can I trust enough to give
up this fight?
Most of me says never. That, like a birthmark,
my mind is made up. Neurological pathways
dug so deep, like a canyon in my cellular
system. Synapses fly faster than the speed of
light and even when I try, I cannot catch them.
Every smile my eyes are gifted with is tainted.
Like watercolors, beautiful, smudged, mixing to
grey, and then black.
Love is amazing. But it hurts. Because you
never know when it will leave. By choice or by
chance.
Cheat the system, my brain tells me. If I love
none, then I will lose none. When it is said and
done.
But my heart knows, it knows that is no way to
live.
"Better to have loved and lost than to never love
at all" rings through my mind. I do not know if I
agree.

You see, I have lost. We have lost. And what is more painful than that?

My mind, like a revolving door takes every love I have and prepares it for its way out.

Thoughts stab against my skull repeatedly. Irrational solutions present themselves, shining and golden. Shaking my head and rubbing my nose will surely do something about that, no? Slicing my skin will surely keep things the way they are, no? Okay, then distraction. Ignoring. Leave me alone, leave me alone! My heart cannot take the weight of love, if only because the weight of fear is heavier. Or perhaps it is a drain? Swallowing up every bit of light that shines my way. I would like to think I was not born this way. That a two hour old anxious, obsessive compulsive, depressive baby did not feel these feelings. I hope she felt endless love. The trust in life and the possibility of forever. I hope no one told her that she would lose that trust in life, her trust in love. I hope her fear was small. I want to be her again. I want to love endlessly. I want to love freely.

pt. 4

5

You're there, eyes wide open in a stare
Your hair, topping your head like a flare.
And I love it.
You laugh when you're nervous,
smile when you cry,
you sleep when you're stressed,
and no one knows why.
And I love it.
You're here when they're there,
you'll do any dare,
you hug like a bear,
and I love it.

On Translating Battles with Mental Illness, pt. 1

It's hell in here.
Each breath is another mouthful of sand,
crystalizing in your throat.
Sight is kaleidoscoped.
Faces are shattered mirrors, reflecting old
dreams.
The oceans are so clear, but the mud on the
beach prevents more than two steps.
Fibers of broken glass stick to your fingers.
Delicately ripping you apart with every
movement, every touch.
Reflections of your hopes flutter through the
humid, dense air.
The knots in your stomach tie you to your bed at
night while the monsters creep towards your
bed.
Every time you make progress, your knees
buckle and your face hits hard on the rising
cement of the constant hill you're climbing.
Your ears bleed from the profanities you scream
out.
But you keep going.
Because once you reach the top of this
never-ending hill, you will breathe fresh air,

touch the smiles of loved ones' faces,
and tie up the monsters with the knots they put
in your stomach.

pt. 2

You're not supposed to get out of here.
It doesn't want you to.
It doesn't let you.
The mask it puts over itself appeals to you.
The mask it puts over your eyes is starting to
stick
dissolve
and stay.
You radiate light, yet all you see is dark.
It's twisted your thought
maimed your sight.
You no longer see what is true
what is bright
what is you.

pt. 3

(FFJF) touch a certain spot (fffffjjjfjfjf)
Or (fjfjfjf j) don't go on at all.
Aaa thought about death deserves a (fjfjfjcjf)
bite (iik) on the lip(dfjkls)
FjFj) rubbed (009aaazaz) my fingers raw.
Did I (kkkm dsxc) break my mother's back?
Give grampa a heart (atataetsdf) attack?
The (dridsfafdasklm;,.) Drip, (ddx) drip, drip of
the sink, sink, sink,
is the(sk,) only thing I can think, think, think
about.
What?(S)
Not (atatesdf) that bad.
(Jkmjklm,j exagge(wrs)rating, joking, (fjdsjfk;x)
pretending
it won't jinx anything.
Try it
Risk it
It's (usdsfsdfkljc) just a paper, write it.
Outstanding excuse.
Center(ffjdskfdscx,i9i) of attention, is that what
you want?
Demonstrate it.
Obsessing
Compulsin(t==g=fcfxdsdcx)g
Disordered(sssxsdx)

pt. 4

I refused to give up on you.
Don't let this hiccup make you lose
sight of who you truly are.
My galaxy's brilliant star.

Don't forget each day is new,
if you're lost then here's a clue:
find your way back home
where your soul is never alone

Like rainbows and clovers
and wishes and daydreams,
their love is all over
never far as it seems.

When dark is greater than the light
and speaking is a burdened plight,
never forget who you are:
my galaxy's brightest star

pt. 5

It latches itself onto you, Its claws wrapped
around your throat.
It is so close to you, all you see is Its face.
Sharp, ripped, inconsistent, ever changing.
Its breath sticks to your lungs, coating them.
In Its eyes is everything.
Old and new.
What was, what is, and endless could-be's
It does not speak but Its essence is ear-piercing.
A cacophony of your own thoughts,
which turn into blades that It holds, poised,
pointed at you.
The irony of being lacerated by concepts of your
own creation,
mutilated by Its twisted sense of humor.
It lifts you off the ground, disorienting you.
You grab the wall behind you, grasping onto
anything.
The sounds, the blades, the sight, your every
nerve is
on fire.
And It remains.
Waiting for you to lose yourself.
And you might.
You might just to survive.

But the wall behind you is there.
That has not moved.
And that remains.
And you hold onto the surface.
Letting it ground you.
Blades hurt less when you stop paying them
attention.
And without your notice It gets bored and at
some point you can breathe,
And your feet find solid ground,
And you walk.
It's still there. It will come back.
But you will endure, and you will persevere
And you will find the ground again.

pt. 6

Bowling alley shoes on a
tight nosed squire.
Ribbons float as the
jester lies.
You bow to dominance,
the queen on her throne.
Her red toed shoes under which
lie souls
of the ones who would not
subject themselves to
her beautiful terror
as her lips curl back
revealing emptiness.
So vast and dark
that the knight falls to his knees and
the most ferocious and
blood-draining battles stop
mid fire.
The silence so strong that your mind is hers
to own,
to control.
You see the souls of those lost,
and the soul that will be
if she is not defeated.
The silence so loud that the

ears of the guilty and
innocent alike bleed out all
they have ever heard.
The jester can't laugh,
or dance,
or sing.
You bow to dominance
to keep your soul,
your laughter,
your song.
The false kingdom,
the card castle will not blow down.
Time will stay stronger
able to keep itself
from being twisted, melted,
pulled into her wallowing
sunken eyes.
So flee.
Flee to another
wax coated paper castle,
where the sun shines on its own,
its rays are not strung to the
frail fingers of the queen but are
free,
and strong.
Able to move on their own.
Where you do not bow to dominance.
The prince, who, like you,
has fled.

Seeing the vast, vile,
empty powers of his
sick, power obese mother.
His feet are bare.
Under which lies soil and seeds.
His smile is his own,
no queen's tremendous features there.
Your mind is your own.
He knows it, and sees it,
but dares not control it.
These squires can unwind.
Knights will stand.
And jesters will sing.

On Translating what it is to Be, pt. 1

I am air.
Light,
playful,
melodic.
I move,
bring,
frolic,
and tickle.
I am air.
Powerful,
invisible,
unbreakable.
I shift,
bend,
howl,
and twist.
I am air.
Widespread,
traveling,
necessary.

pt. 2

I am earth.
Supportive,
strong,
steady.
I hold,
mold,
provide,
and grow. I am earth.
Fractured,
untamed,
uneven.
I quake,
shift,
crumble,
and roll.
I am earth.
Nature,
home,
necessary.

pt. 2

I am fire.
Warm,
dancing,
mesmerizing.
I heat,
light,
protect,
and cook.
I am fire.
Hot,
ever changing,
unpredictable.
I burn,
alter,
expand,
and take.
I am fire.
Bold,
renewing,
necessary.

pt. 3

I am water.
Still,
tame,
balanced.
I hold,
carry,
transport,
and reflect.
I am water
wild
forceful
ebbing and flowing.
I push and pull,
change,
churn,
and crash.
I am water.
Endless,
precious,
necessary.

pt. 4

We are all just people, aren't we?
In fact, yes, we are.
But there is more to it.
We are made up of moments and interactions,
of relationships and beliefs.
We have all grown from toothless wobblers.
Held onto some aspects of youth, losing others.
We absentmindedly do things only our way.
Move our hands our way, laugh our way. laugh
our own way.
It is truly fascinating.
We stand against the wind, hold it,
or let it pass through us, frankly depending on
our mood.

pt. 5

They are broken
    of heart
    of trust
But still they rise
    fight
    chant
    demand
Pulling from the depths of generations
Before them.
Of lives before them.
Persevering beyond what could be
    expected
    hoped for
    asked for.
We no longer beg.
We demand
Command
Rights that do not change by
Skin color.
We ignite
Each other
With passion for what is right
What is human.
A flame spreads its tendrils

Rustling the embers of those of us too long
quiet.
Bursting forth because
WE WILL NOT ACCEPT THIS.
We no longer pity
From the comfort of our living rooms.
Tapping twice on the face of another
Lost victim.
We reach out
Step out
Clasp onto each other and
Protest.
We learn
We grow.
We cannot
Will not
Casually accept
Any longer.

pt. 6

Deafening sound, she laughs so loud, cheering
anything that's down.
Changing beauty, she makes the world perfect,
as everything she touches shines as a star would.
Defying gravity, she leaps from shell to shell
looking for the perfect one, making footprints in
the sand.
Mystifying the Gods, she jumps so high they
could cradle her in their arms so she could
finally touch the sky with her small fingers.
Making bargains with Mother Earth, she
re-plants a dead flower in hopes it would grow
to be as tall as she.
Tricking fiction, she promises that she sees a
mermaid and makes sure to let me know they
will meet again.
Forgetting logic, she kisses the sun goodnight
and tucks it in under a blanket of stars.
Jumping through time, she slips her small hand
in mine and tells me that she is going to grow up
to be an angel.
Wishing on the first star, she asks for the flower
to grow.
Greeting the stars, she makes sure to name all of
them. Pleasing the moon, she tells it a story.

Drifting on only the softest clouds, she finally
closes her eyes.
Pleading with sleep, she is already hoping for
tomorrow.

pt. 7

I am bigger than my skin.
I span time
and places
and dimensions.
I am all that is and will be of this lifetime and
I carry myself in this body.
Potential rests in my very joints, bones, and
cells.
In the cracks between my teeth and the fibers of
my muscles.
Breath reaches every space in my body, pushing
light,
expelling the unnecessary.
I am 31,
and 2,
and 16, all in one.
I am,
was,
and will be.
Light, in shades and colors undetectable by the
human eye
radiates from my body.
My power is endless, if I put my
body, mind, and soul into it.
I am capable.

I am able.
I am potential energy.

On Translating Gratitude

27

Thank you for being.
Being you.
Being there to help me get through so much I
never thought I would.
Thank you for seeing.
Seeing what's inside too.
Thank you for knowing.
Knowing for me when I can't explain what I'm
thinking.
Thank you for showing.
Showing me all that's worthwhile and lovely.
Thank you for loving.
Loving when I felt like I couldn't.
Thank you for hugging.
Holding me up when I couldn't on my own.

On Translating
Miscellaneous Musings

I'll be where
the hills fall into the sky,
and fish walk onto the shore.
Where stars stumble into the river
and go for a swim.
Where trees bend and twist
just to get you higher.
And kisses are fireflies
touching your nose.
Where songs are the steps from
one place to another.
I'll be there.

On Translating a Silly Jaunt

I'm so fragile, they call me sir rammick
Say the wrong thing, I just might panic
I'm literal
Lyrical
Outright hysterical
I'll ask you one more time,
Though I know it's not logical.
I'm medicated
Educated
Laugh so loud, haters get sonicated
Tales of my puns from near to far are predicated.
Dedicated
Feelin love from my friends, got me so elevated.
Obsessive
Compulsive
Disordered
Depressive
Sometimes it gets excessive.
But I know that I am held
By the people that I meld
with. We care so hard
people think it's mythic.
All pros no cons
Transparent like chiffon
The list goes on and on

And
On and
On

www.ingramcontent.com/pod-product-compliance
Lightning Source LLC
LaVergne TN
LVHW010933200726
843509LV00013B/2196